Night
Swimming

Noelle Darilek

Night Swimming

Introduction

I spent a lot of time wishing I could write beautiful words, while also reading a great deal of them. Something inside me kept calling me to write the book.

I've had lines pop into my head unannounced, watched ideas be born from inspiration and things that struck me, recorded awkward voice memos on my phone while driving, and left my journal on my nightstand, just in case.

I've gathered some of these words and thoughts born from my feelings and experiences and bound the best ones together. My hope is that they strike you like they did me when we first bumped into each other so long ago.

Sit with them and sip them like a nice cup of something warm and simply enjoy.

You wrecked my perfect world and I love you
more for it.

The seeds of your speech took root in my chest. The stems twisted and twined around my ribcage, flower petals bloomed and spilled from my mouth. The sweetest longing in my chest for the glowing bits of light that formed constellations and strands of stars in your mouth. The magnetic force between our lips, drawing them closer.

After giving you everything I held in my hands, I couldn't understand why yours were still empty.

– *what is enough?*

She'll never see
your fickle freckled
summer skin
I stroked
on lazy
afternoons
in bed,
or your
deep dimples
hidden beneath
your winter
coat
on the
smooth
face
I held
in my
hands.

– *her*

Untangling messy words
and
rearranging
spare thoughts;
words your lips
have spoken
as many stars
as there are
in the sky.
The lazy sun
tumbles
behind
the languid moon,
and the
glow
of the
ultraviolet
light
illuminates
the thin
horizon
behind
the sea.

— *closure*

Musings

We went to the museum late one spring
night as the moon hung high above us.

There was an event being held and the small
space was glowing. There were people salsa
dancing to live music under purple and
orange lights beneath what looked like a
giant, flowery, ribcage hanging from the
ceiling. There were people strolling upstairs
looking at art, stopping at different pieces,
and couples holding hands.

You and I wandered from room to room
looking at paintings and sculptures and
installations while I pretended to know what
they all meant.

My favorite piece was a blue neon sign that
catches your eye when you walk up the
stairs.

With scroll letters it reads, "Webelonghere"
with the words completely connected.

You are here. We are here. We belong here.
Together. You are here and exactly here. You
don't need to be anywhere else. You don't
belong anywhere else or with anyone else.

No one will ever
hold your heart
the way
my
capable hands
did.
No one will ever
know you
the way
the
buzzing universe
inside me
did
when it
collided happily
with yours.
No one will share
our stories
our laughs
our memories
(so fragile now)
the way
we did.
Sometimes
just knowing
that you
loved me
is
enough.

— *comfort / the way*

The poised lion spoke to the shy swan with a sureness that made her believe she could be anyone and say anything. His sleepy breath laced with a pungent trace of whiskey from the night before, she took his tangled words and combed through the knots. He took her weedy words from her messy head and turned them into vines that bore beautiful, scrumptious fruit. They spoke in a way that felt like sitting by the warmth of a fire while the snowflakes take their time falling to the barren earth.

– *nineteen*

Don't discount your memories
because you found someone sweeter —
what you had when you had it
was exactly what you wanted

You loved and you gave
and went on great adventures,
you had hard times
and sad times,
but laughter
and sunshine

Just because you see
the memories differently now,
doesn't mean
that what they are
at their core
has changed at all

I miss your sweet
interruptions
but
once upon a time
doesn't always end
with happily ever
after
and hearts
and dreams
tend
to shatter.

A million words of our story, once clearly laid out in plain and neat rows on bound and covered pages in black and white; all of these words inevitably pulled down by gravity now lie in an indiscernible blackened mess and mass of letters at the bottom of clean, blank pages. The words of our story are still bound and covered, but you can no longer make out exactly what they say. What do they all mean anyway?

– *gravity*

Cruising down the boulevard
the magic seeps out
of the speakers
and dances into my ears.
You grab my hand
and steer with the other.
You pull me closer
at a red light.
You wrap me
in your arms,
my head cocked
and gently resting
on your chest.
I can barely make out
the glowing city lights
that disappear
behind headlights
over your dash.
No plans, no nothing –
the perfect moment,
just us together.
This feeling of utterly
pure bliss
holding our hearts
tethered together.

– *like real people do*

"I promise I won't hurt you," you plead, but roses say the same thing before its thorns make you bleed.

What did she do (and I not) to your warm-blooded, tender heart that made you hold your sweet honey and rose petals over my head?

Dishes stay
in the sink,
lips stay
buzzing
and chapped.
Sleeping hours
stay
small.
Thoughts
stay filled
to the brim.
Laundry stays
piled high
and
bedsheets
stay messy.
You stay
a little longer
when I'm
with
you.

— cause and effect / sign of the times

"Please come."

My reply was admission to a night of hilarity and shiny scenes that crept into the early hours of the morning.

— my favorite memory

Everything I never said

It's a peculiar thing when you are suddenly
uprooted from a situation. One day not too
long after, you are forced to take a step back
and look back on the stretch of time that has
passed since the day your life shifted in
nearly a blink. To look back on the entirety
of a film after the credits have rolled, and to
walk out of the theater and see more clearly
the story and all of its intricacies, and see
how all of the strands were woven together
to create this plot and this grand story. To
see what you couldn't see when you were
there living it, watching it happen, and
unfold in front of you. To see what was there
all along, but that you were blind to or
simply stored someplace in your mind where
you would forget about it. But these things
were always there. Regardless.

These pockets in my mind I tried to fill with
justifications, these craters I hoped would be
filled with stardust, these precipices that
only got steeper. These things that lingered
and made a home in my head, everything my
voice could never spill and my mouth could
never form – these are those things.

Sitting up on a pedestal was not a
comfortable place to be. Sitting there clothed
in standards left over from a past you have

yet to pass and pressures that left me feeling unsettled and dizzy. Sitting there glued to the seat early on, reaching for standards just out of arms reach. Reaching to pick from a tree, traits that weren't quite ripe enough yet. I sat there and saw myself do my best to attain them and take a bite of the hard fruit. I watched my confidence crumble with every bite. You must know, the fruit will ripen and the flowers will yield to the sun and bloom where they grow, when watered, in their own time.

Time wears many hats and time is crucial. Time played an interesting role. It passed and passed and waited patiently for us to catch up with it, but it kept moving forward and we continually slowed. Time showed me that I cared for you, deeply, and that I was attentive to you, recklessly. It bore on and on endlessly and ceaselessly and wore my selfless soul thin. To pour yourself into someone, into something, to give away and spend every last cent of your affection, and to get back the sentiment that you still missed the mark, that it wasn't enough, that the judges didn't clap but turned away. But it was all you had to give away. To feel like a fool for giving too much, wondering if your love is too much, to get glimpses and peeks into a wonderful place on a rare occasion, to beg for affection, to give and not get.

To define feeling loved, for me, is a feeling of wholeness. It is to know the entirety of someone from every angle and vantage point. To know the nooks and crannies of their minds, to walk into dusty, dark attics and to swim in clear blue, sun-kissed waters with them. To hold someone in your hands and know the universe buzzing inside their warm body and to kiss their flaws and cradle their strengths. To love and love again regardless of crashing waves and crumbling crags. To be met with a barrier, to not have the key to all of the locked doors, is disheartening. To yearn to know echoes of an existence and to be met with a door that leads to a cluttered space filled with dusty picture frames, melodies playing from an old record, creaks in the floor, initials carved into wooden tables, letters tucked away in trunks, that mean nothing to you.

The bluest spot of them all, the regret that will dwell, that the tiny sparks and flickers never grew into flames, but turned to ash in the night. That you, nor I, ever hit our highest potential simultaneously. That maybe if I'd known it all along, I could have stepped back and reached a little higher. Something that almost was. Something that could have been. Something that never will be.

People ask if we'll get back together. I tell them, "*no.*" Because wolves don't starve when there's nothing to eat.

— full moon

I want a love where La Vie En Rose is
constantly playing on repeat in my swirling
head behind a pair of sparkling blue eyes. I
want the fresh smell of crisp Paris baguettes
in the air and a slow dance by the Seine at
sunset as the Tower glitters across the
water, the lights reflecting onto the river and
lighting up the setting sky, while my head
rests gracefully on your shoulder. I want a
love like La Vie En Rose; classic and
beautiful, willingly giving in to the feeling
that you've found something close to magic.

– *what will be*

Sitting across the table from you,
your face older,
your head fuller
of sweet memories.
I look across
the cheap white linen
covering the wobbly,
wooden table
and smile,
as big as the sea,
back at you.
9 PM on a Sunday,
free soup,
and just us in here.
I swat away a fly
from my face
and you do the same.
I laugh
as I take a bite
of a too-cheesy slice
of falling-apart
and too garlicy pizza.
I make a mess
and we laugh
as I experience
for a moment
pure
and unfiltered
bliss
in our little paradise.

— *where the love goes / perfect places*

I cried you an ocean
and picked you a garden of roses,
all so I could get back
a handful of loose change,
and a secondhand heart.

If
a trillion
cells
in our
warm-
blooded,
electric
bodies
can get
along,
then why
can't
we?

His words dripped like honey from the beehive on a hot summer day. His sticky, slurry speech whispered in my ear though the 2 AM summer silence. My back pressed lustfully between the wall and the weight of his body, he tells me once more the poetry he spoke so gently all night. My jeweled clip-on earring lies on the pavement like Cinderella's forgotten slipper, and he pulls me closer as the honey drips.

— *"monsieur, une autre bouteille de vin s'il vous plaît"*

I may have started the fire, but when I tried
to put it out, you poured the gasoline.

   — the truth

I
don't know
how you wandered
into my life,
how you waltzed
into my ballroom,
took me
by the
hand,
and asked
for a dance.
But
I wish
you'd wander
back in
with your heart
a little softer
and your eyes
a little older.
I wish
we were
strangers
and I'd
meet you
over coffee
and you'd spill
your soul
to me,
like cream
overtakes coffee,
and I'd absorb
your sweet sugar

eagerly.
We'd look
at each other,
with adoring eyes,
knowing we'd found
a slice
of something
sparkling.
We'd unwrap
each part
of each
other
like a
present
on Christmas morning
and gape
in awe
at our treasure.
We'd be so
unapologetically
ourselves
with no reservations,
and dance
along the galaxy
until
the sky
goes black.

– second chances

My fingertips whisper, "I miss you," under fresh sheets; my outstretched arms aching for the warm body that laid beside me.

— *12:26 am: trying to fall asleep*

There are not
quite
enough words
in the
English
language
to adequately
and
accurately
express
how
I feel
about
you.

– speechless

Lazily
greeting
the world
as it
gently opens
its eyes.
Quick kisses
and
long kisses
and
tossing beneath
the sheets.
Biscuits and gravy,
coffee
and eggs
over easy;
sleepily
making conversation.
The day
you nervously
uttered
three words
all those weeks
ago.

– *Sundays*

And maybe the silence means that you know we'll see each other again and we'll talk to glowing faces about all of the silence we kept secret from each other for so long.

— *perspective*

What happens to the love
when two hearts break?
Where does it go?
It stays
and lingers
in your bedsheets
in your hair
on your skin
on your fridge.
It slowly packs
its large suitcase
full of photos
full of roses
full of love letters
and records.
It picks up its things
one day
and leaves quietly
in the night
while you rest your head,
beneath your bedsheets.
It sneaks out the door
and tiptoes across
the floor.
It leaves the house key
under the mat
and a note on
the door, thanking you
for its stay.
You wake up one morning
but the love has moved
into your memories and

found a new place to settle
in your heart.
Love will come back one day
(you know)
but when is a mystery
yet to be answered.
And when love does,
it will be shiny
and new,
it will be the love
that's been waiting for you.

This
insatiable,
lustrous,
illuminated
love,
races
whimsically
through
our veins.

Give yourself room to grow;
plant your feet on fertile soil
somewhere spacious and sunny.
Don't pry the petals open,
they will yield to the sun with water and
care,
in their own time.

You'll always
be with
me
in some
capacity –
in an
ounce
or
a
pound,
in a
basket
of roses
or a weed
in a field,
in a flicker
of a memory,
or the hairs
on the back of
my neck
standing on end –
you'll always be
with me.

– *first love*

You lived in a fairytale
in a dream world
overgrown with daisies
the sky bursting
with stars.
You danced on the moon
and swam
at the bottom
of the sea.
You turned your axis
a little closer
to the sun
and fought
what gravity does.
You spewed your heart
your honey
your stardust
your tears.
You wrapped your love
up in a galaxy
and prayed
it would shine
forever.
What you had escaped
and snuck out
the back door.
It left you alone
and alone again.
You vowed to never
again
let it in – let the
light

fully in,
let it shine
through the cracks
in your heart.
Because something hiding
in the nooks
and crannies
always pulled
the shades
back down.
Something still calls
you
home,
some forgotten
lost voicemail
some love letters
from
a century ago
someone who pulls
you back
like the tide
pulls the moon –
you'll always stay

– don't make me say her name.

Suddenly it was summer and the balminess of your sunshine warmed my cold skin. Your cool night air that replaces the sunset sends chills down my spine and I fall for you completely as I abandon a season that did me no good.

— summer ends / summer starts

A hint
of intoxication
on our breaths,
we spew our
souls
until they're
laying
on
the bed
next to us.
The remains
of us;
the tiny pieces
we pick up
and try
to
figure out
how to fit them
together now.
Holding
the other's
heart
up with our
gaze –
a moment
meant for
just us;
a moment
so naked
and raw
it could
only

be us
in our most
true form.

I want to crawl back
to that place on my knees
where the freckles
on your face
are more pronounced
in the morning
light
and where the first thing
I see
when I wake
is you
still asleep
underneath
my bedsheets.

— *homesick*

Loving you is like swan diving into the deep
end and slowly rising to the surface.
It's seeing the night sky shimmer and
sparkle as clear as it's ever been and taking
your time tracing each constellation.
It's forehead kisses as light and fleeting as
the flap of a butterfly's wing and it's having
room and taking time for just us to share and
savor the space we're in.

– night swimming

I throw the feeling back over the horizon
with all of my might.
I watch it disappear and grow smaller until I
can no longer make out its shape.
I awake one day to find the feeling lying
there beside me – no cuts or bruises, looking
shiny and new as before.
I let it stay for a little while longer until I
shoo it out the door again.
But it's no matter – for a day or two from
now it will be knocking hard and loud.

– *boomerang*

You took a heart
with you when
you left
(mine)
and left me
with one
too
(yours).
I cradled it
and held it
close
as we reveled
in
our memories.

Pinky promise I'll always be yours.
Pinky promise a piece of me will always
forever be with you.
Pinky promise no matter what, you won't
forget a single sliver of me, of us.
Pinky promise when my sharp edges snag
you and when my smooth skin kisses you,
you'll love me just the same.
Pinky promise to cradle my heart and carry
it close to yours.
Pinky promise you'll tell me every day I
mean a million shiny stars to you.
Pinky promise you won't let us fall and you'll
bide your time for me.
Pinky promise I'll always be yours.

Mon amour chéri

Light peaking,
sneaking
underneath
eyelids

Flutter
lashes;
gaze up – a
perfect portrait

Warm
limbs
messed
with mine

Steady,
bottomless breathing;
your sturdy frame
under mine

Sleepy hands
search –
fingertips spew
sparks (down my spine)

My restless
ribcage
full of
flicker

Leaden lids
lock yours;
flesh parts
over skin

Closer

I would lasso the
crescent moon
for you
and place the halo
on your head;
rearrange the stars
and constellations,
just to doze with
you in bed.

I would bare
my soul to you,
naked and raw;
show you all
the fragments,
and show you all
the flaws.

I would interlace
your fingers
where there's space;
shotgun, 10-and-2 –
it's you, I adore.
I would feel
your chest
rise and fall
while I stay up
and while you snore.

I would make you

mix CDs,
and keep a list
of memories.
I would play our song
on full blast,
and leave the others
in the past.

I would allow myself
not to run,
and not steal
your heart,
simply for fun,
no matter how
dear to mine
yours gets
over time.

I left you in a train station
before the sun came up;
I didn't even look back
because I knew you wouldn't.

I met you in a crowded room,
surrounded by strangers
drinking beer;
I left a piece of me,
I left it there.

All those promises we made —
how we'd always be there,
how we'd always stay —
our greatest fear realized
by our own doings.

What happened to us?
Where did that spark
run off to? I thought I
folded down the corner
of this page to return to.

But I've lost my place
and have no memory
of where we left
off or what
I'm reading now.

I'd try to find it,
but it's no use at all;
that moment,

that chapter
is over and
will never be back.

Off a backroad in a prairie
sits a little log cabin
nestled beneath mountain tips
bathed in lavender light
and drizzled with wildflowers.

There sits a house with
a flickering front porch light
that flips on each evening
as the sunlight fills the valley
and the rambling river.

The light is left on each night
for you when you get lost in
the darkness, lingering in my
heart, looking for your way
back home.

It shines till dawn
and with open arms,
I will welcome you each
dusk, when you've lost your
way, and need a safe place
to rest.

You know the way back home,
the path is worn
and overgrown;
you've traced the map's lines
over
and over again –
the pull of the compass

lures you back.

– home in my heart

Swirl your car
up
to the
top
of the parking
garage roof

Put it
in park
and roll
the windows
low

A spark
as the sun
lowers,
unclick our belts;
the balmy
breeze
tangled with hits
of Mary

Sharing secrets
and
sharing laughter;
old classic tunes
floating through
your speakers

Dreaming of leaving
it all behind
and moving to

LA;
countless nights
spent
this way

— *how summer passed*

The strawberry moon
was low and faded,
like lovers that linger
until dawn

I clung to you
like a lifeboat,
far from shore,
and dreamt one day
of setting sail

I think you truly saved me
when I needed someone most;
as the exception to everything,
we willingly became inseparable

Sometimes I still think
we'll find each other again,
(one day)
when we've each grown up
just a little bit more

When regret taps at my window,
very late at night,
I remember the first time we kissed —
how the world melted away;

How we could be the
only two people
in a crowded restaurant,
and how electrified
and connected
our souls were

The past creeps in
this time of year
as the summer takes
its final bow

The false anticipation
of fall
and change
and magic wearing off

But despite the pain
last fall bore,
I remember too
there was something more

Amidst the fears
and between my tears
I stumbled into you

I found an angel
and someone true,
to make my heart
begin anew

So now this fall
I'll remember not,
my heart in pieces
but you there,
the twist in plot

– *angel*

And after all this time,
unwrapping
our memories
is still a wound
that has yet
to heal
fully
and still
stings
with pain

You're "I will,
I will,"
but you won't,
you won't

You're a far away,
missed call
at 3 AM,
at 4

You're a one last time,
a long-distance voice,
a can't-keep-it promise,
from an ocean away

You're a summer track,
parking lot,
sticky, sweaty, summer, at sunset,
with strappy water sandals

You're a little-too-late note,
hidden in your dash;
slow it down dear,
now, don't go slow

You're six months of silence,
too busy to care;
space for the best,
mistake of the year

You're a shot of whiskey,
but not too many;

warm and electric,
oh baby, just kiss me

You're not what I want,
but just what I need;
too close,
then too far

You're pancakes and coffee,
French fries and ice cream;
twenty plus questions,
and sweep-you-off-your-feet hugs

You're laughing too hard,
calls from the 10th floor,
thunderstorms,
and talking in your car

You're 19 and counting?
Tipsy and kind,
Texas summer nights, shotgun,
and Multiply

— you

Perched
high above
the world,
you sing
sweet songs
of past lovers —
those living
and each one
before —
but never once
do you sing
my song
I sung
so softly
for months

  — *mockingbird*

Find me in another life
and scream my name loud

Tear open the skies
and let the rain pour;
flood the streets
and fill the sky with
lighting streaks

Crumble the crags
and steepen the precipices
and I'll know this time
it was you all along
who would shelter my heart
and keep me safe
from the storm

We're like a wildfire out west atop the
mountains at night — beautiful and
dangerous; costly and sparkling.
Orange glitter against a cobalt night sky;
smoke filling the air with the smell of
burning sweet pines.
Very late at night, the trees will keep
burning and never, not ever, will they lose
their shine until everything around them has
turned to ash.

— *wildfire*

When I was younger, I used to believe the birds flying together in clusters across the sky or a single bird perched on my windowsill were signs from God that He was watching over me.

These days as the sun sinks below the horizon and turns the clouds into glowing pink cotton candy floss, I see the possibilities it presents and breathe its sweet perfume.

....

I wish we could run away together (you and I) to some faraway place where the sun always shines and that's close to the ocean, or where the mountains stand tall and the winters are full of snow.

I'd wait tables at a highway diner with a neon sign out front, serving hot coffee to locals and strangers on sticky vinyl table covers. I'd write about our adventures in our new home and make burnt grilled cheeses for us after work late at night.

You'd write your script all day and pitch ideas to important people, waiting to catch a break while working on sets of small productions. You'd play video games while the light of the TV lures me to sleep before

coming to bed and make me your special
scrambled eggs very early in the morning.

We'd tie our lives together like a pretty pink
ribbon on top of a present and intertwine our
new lives together until we finally both find
our way, living off of what we can until we
get exactly there and sharing the sweetest
sap of the moments together until we do.

– dusk / the best times

Staring into
your bright
blue eyes
overcome
with peace
and affection,
the background
is blurry
and all
I can see
is you

– how I finally understood what true love is
/ magic

and in the end,
the wind
made a
terrible pull, and
brought
with it
a new tide.

Table of Contents

About Me

Noelle is a recent graduate from the University of Texas. She currently resides in Austin, where she grew up. She enjoys reading, writing, and traveling the world in her free time.

Contact:

noelledarilek@gmail.com

Printed in the USA
CPSIA information can be obtained
at www.ICGtesting.com
CBHW071205230724
12031CB00030B/246